THE PHILLIP KEVEREN SERIES   PIANO SOLO

CHRISTMAS AT THE MOVIES

— PIANO LEVEL —
LATE INTERMEDIATE/EARLY ADVANCED

ISBN 978-1-4584-0774-0

HAL•LEONARD®
CORPORATION

7777 W. BLUEMOUND RD. P.O. BOX 13819 MILWAUKEE, WI 53213

Visit Hal Leonard Online at
www.halleonard.com

Visit Phillip at
www.phillipkeveren.com

PREFACE

Christmas-themed movies are a beloved part of seasonal traditions, and the music in these films plays a significant part in their appeal. This collection of piano solos features evergreens alongside newer songs that will likely be with us for a long time.

A suggested *Christmas at the Movies Suite*: Play the first four selections in succession ("Overture," "My Favorite Things," "Count Your Blessings Instead of Sheep," "We Need a Little Christmas"). You will find the pacing to be just right for a holiday medley.

"Carol for Another Christmas" is a stocking stuffer from me to you that was not written expressly for a film. I feel it fits right in, however, as it was composed by one of the titans of movie music, Henry Mancini.

Merry Christmas!
Phillip Keveren

BIOGRAPHY

Phillip Keveren, a multi-talented keyboard artist and composer, has composed original works in a variety of genres from piano solo to symphonic orchestra. Mr. Keveren gives frequent concerts and workshops for teachers and their students in the United States, Canada, Europe, and Asia. Mr. Keveren holds a B.M. in composition from California State University Northridge and a M.M. in composition from the University of Southern California.

CONTENTS

OVERTURE
from the Twentieth Century Fox Feature Film MIRACLE ON 34th STREET

By BRUCE BROUGHTON
Arranged by Phillip Keveren

Majestically (♩ = 104)

Joyfully (♩ = 120)

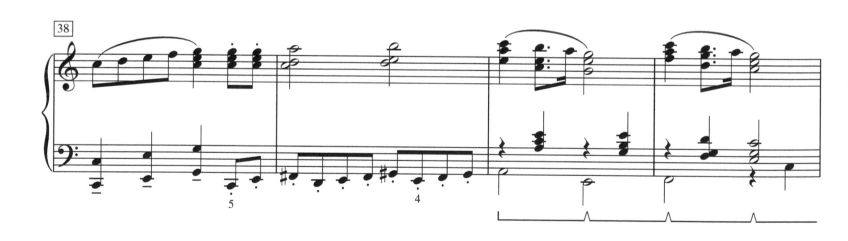

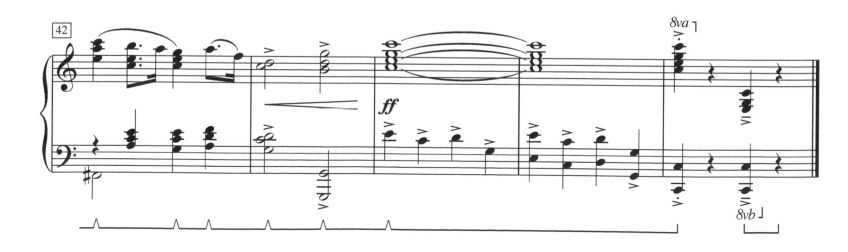

MY FAVORITE THINGS
from THE SOUND OF MUSIC

Lyrics by OSCAR HAMMERSTEIN II
Music by RICHARD RODGERS
Arranged by Phillip Keveren

Lively Waltz (♩ = 176–184)

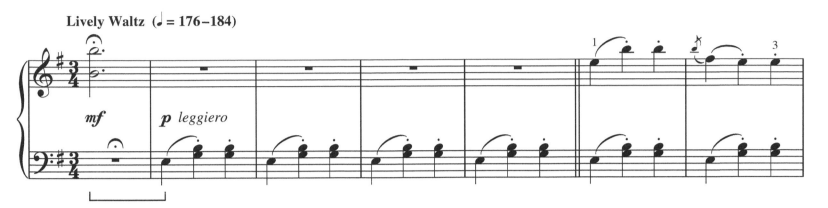

COUNT YOUR BLESSINGS
INSTEAD OF SHEEP

from the Motion Picture Irving Berlin's WHITE CHRISTMAS

Words and Music by
IRVING BERLIN
Arranged by Phillip Keveren

WE NEED A LITTLE CHRISTMAS

from MAME

Music and Lyric by
JERRY HERMAN
Arranged by Phillip Keveren

Bright show tempo (♩ = 126)

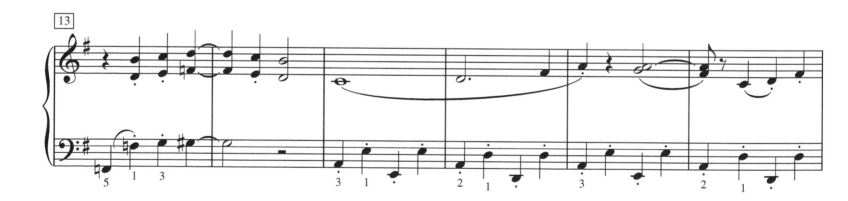

GOD BLESS US EVERYONE

from Disney's A CHRISTMAS CAROL

Words and Music by ALAN SILVESTRI
and GLEN BALLARD
Arranged by Phillip Keveren

BABY, IT'S COLD OUTSIDE

from the Motion Picture NEPTUNE'S DAUGHTER

By FRANK LOESSER
Arranged by Phillip Keveren

HAPPY HOLIDAY
from the Motion Picture Irving Berlin's HOLIDAY INN

Words and Music by
IRVING BERLIN
Arranged by Phillip Keveren

SALLY'S SONG

from Tim Burton's THE NIGHTMARE BEFORE CHRISTMAS

Music and Lyrics by
DANNY ELFMAN
Arranged by Phillip Keveren

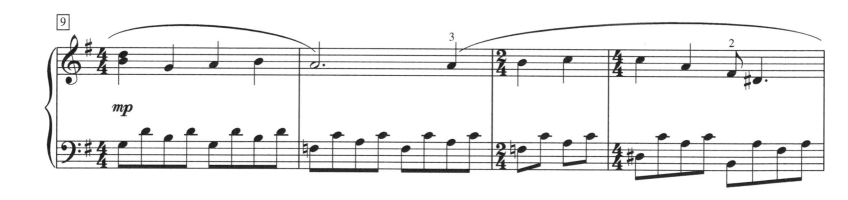

SOMEWHERE IN MY MEMORY

from the Twentieth Century Fox Motion Picture HOME ALONE

Words by LESLIE BRICUSSE
Music by JOHN WILLIAMS
Arranged by Phillip Keveren

28

SILVER BELLS
from the Paramount Picture THE LEMON DROP KID

Words and Music by JAY LIVINGSTON
and RAY EVANS
Arranged by Phillip Keveren

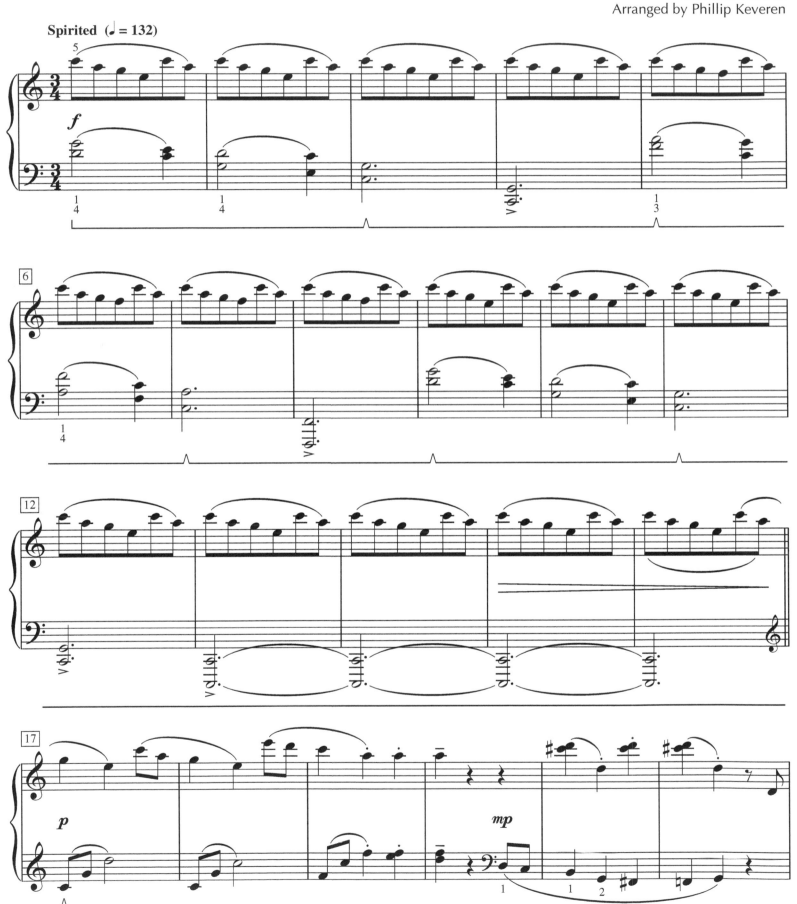

SPIRIT OF THE SEASON
from Warner Bros. Pictures' THE POLAR EXPRESS

Words and Music by GLEN BALLARD
and ALAN SILVESTRI
Arranged by Phillip Keveren

STAR OF BETHLEHEM
from the Twentieth Century Fox Feature Film HOME ALONE

Words by LESLIE BRICUSSE
Music by JOHN WILLIAMS
Arranged by Phillip Keveren

WHERE ARE YOU CHRISTMAS?

from DR. SEUSS' HOW THE GRINCH STOLE CHRISTMAS

Words and Music by WILL JENNINGS,
JAMES HORNER and MARIAH CAREY
Arranged by Phillip Keveren

WHITE CHRISTMAS
from the Motion Picture Irving Berlin's HOLIDAY INN

Words and Music by
IRVING BERLIN
Arranged by Phillip Keveren

Flowing, with great expressive freedom ($\quad$ = 96 – 104)

CAROL FOR ANOTHER CHRISTMAS

By HENRY MANCINI
Arranged by Phillip Keveren

WHEN CHRISTMAS COMES TO TOWN

from Warner Bros. Pictures' THE POLAR EXPRESS

Words and Music by GLEN BALLARD
and ALAN SILVESTRI
Arranged by Phillip Keveren

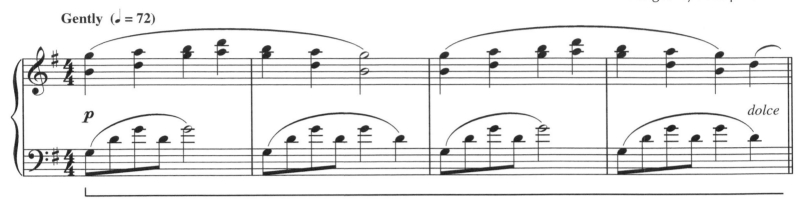

52

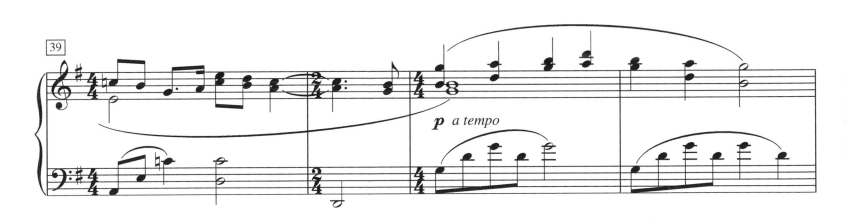

THE PHILLIP KEVEREN SERIES

PIANO SOLO

00156644	**ABBA for Classical Piano**	$15.99
00311024	**Above All**	$12.99
00311348	**Americana**	$12.99
00198473	**Bach Meets Jazz**	$14.99
00313594	**Bacharach and David**	$15.99
00306412	**The Beatles**	$17.99
00312189	**The Beatles for Classical Piano**	$16.99
00275876	**The Beatles – Recital Suites**	$19.99
00312546	**Best Piano Solos**	$15.99
00156601	**Blessings**	$12.99
00198656	**Blues Classics**	$12.99
00284359	**Broadway Songs with a Classical Flair**	$14.99
00310669	**Broadway's Best**	$14.99
00312106	**Canzone Italiana**	$12.99
00280848	**Carpenters**	$16.99
00310629	**A Celtic Christmas**	$12.99
00310549	**The Celtic Collection**	$12.95
00280571	**Celtic Songs with a Classical Flair**	$12.99
00263362	**Charlie Brown Favorites**	$14.99
00312190	**Christmas at the Movies**	$14.99
00294754	**Christmas Carols with a Classical Flair**	$12.99
00311414	**Christmas Medleys**	$14.99
00236669	**Christmas Praise Hymns**	$12.99
00233788	**Christmas Songs for Classical Piano**	$12.99
00311769	**Christmas Worship Medleys**	$14.99
00310607	**Cinema Classics**	$15.99
00301857	**Circles**	$10.99
00311101	**Classic Wedding Songs**	$10.95
00311292	**Classical Folk**	$10.95
00311083	**Classical Jazz**	$12.95
00137779	**Coldplay for Classical Piano**	$16.99
00311103	**Contemporary Wedding Songs**	$12.99
00348788	**Country Songs with a Classical Flair**	$14.99
00249097	**Disney Recital Suites**	$17.99
00311754	**Disney Songs for Classical Piano**	$17.99
00241379	**Disney Songs for Ragtime Piano**	$17.99
00311881	**Favorite Wedding Songs**	$14.99
00315974	**Fiddlin' at the Piano**	$12.99
00311811	**The Film Score Collection**	$15.99
00269408	**Folksongs with a Classical Flair**	$12.99
00144353	**The Gershwin Collection**	$14.99
00233789	**Golden Scores**	$14.99
00144351	**Gospel Greats**	$12.99
00183566	**The Great American Songbook**	$12.99
00312084	**The Great Melodies**	$12.99
00311157	**Great Standards**	$12.95
00171621	**A Grown-Up Christmas List**	$12.99
00311071	**The Hymn Collection**	$12.99
00311349	**Hymn Medleys**	$12.99

00280705	**Hymns in a Celtic Style**	$12.99
00269407	**Hymns with a Classical Flair**	$12.99
00311249	**Hymns with a Touch of Jazz**	$12.99
00310905	**I Could Sing of Your Love Forever**	$12.95
00310762	**Jingle Jazz**	$14.99
00175310	**Billy Joel for Classical Piano**	$16.99
00126449	**Elton John for Classical Piano**	$16.99
00310839	**Let Freedom Ring!**	$12.99
00238988	**Andrew Lloyd Webber Piano Songbook**	$14.99
00313227	**Andrew Lloyd Webber Solos**	$15.99
00313523	**Mancini Magic**	$16.99
00312113	**More Disney Songs for Classical Piano**	$16.99
00311295	**Motown Hits**	$14.99
00300640	**Piano Calm**	$12.99
00339131	**Piano Calm: Christmas**	$12.99
00346009	**Piano Calm: Prayer**	$14.99
00306870	**Piazzolla Tangos**	$16.99
00156645	**Queen for Classical Piano**	$15.99
00310755	**Richard Rodgers Classics**	$16.99
00289545	**Scottish Songs**	$12.99
00310609	**Shout to the Lord!**	$14.99
00119403	**The Sound of Music**	$14.99
00311978	**The Spirituals Collection**	$10.99
00210445	**Star Wars**	$16.99
00224738	**Symphonic Hymns for Piano**	$14.99
00279673	**Tin Pan Alley**	$12.99
00312112	**Treasured Hymns for Classical Piano**	$14.99
00144926	**The Twelve Keys of Christmas**	$12.99
00278486	**The Who for Classical Piano**	$16.99
00294036	**Worship with a Touch of Jazz**	$12.99
00311911	**Yuletide Jazz**	$17.99

EASY PIANO

00210401	**Adele for Easy Classical Piano**	$15.99
00310610	**African-American Spirituals**	$10.99
00218244	**The Beatles for Easy Classical Piano**	$14.99
00218387	**Catchy Songs for Piano**	$12.99
00310973	**Celtic Dreams**	$12.99
00233686	**Christmas Carols for Easy Classical Piano**	$12.99
00311126	**Christmas Pops**	$14.99
00311548	**Classic Pop/Rock Hits**	$14.99
00310769	**A Classical Christmas**	$10.95
00310975	**Classical Movie Themes**	$12.99
00144352	**Disney Songs for Easy Classical Piano**	$12.99
00311093	**Early Rock 'n' Roll**	$14.99
00311997	**Easy Worship Medleys**	$12.99
00289547	**Duke Ellington**	$14.99
00160297	**Folksongs for Easy Classical Piano**	$12.99

00110374	**George Gershwin Classics**	$12.99
00310805	**Gospel Treasures**	$12.99
00306821	**Vince Guaraldi Collection**	$19.99
00160294	**Hymns for Easy Classical Piano**	$12.99
00310798	**Immortal Hymns**	$12.99
00311294	**Jazz Standards**	$12.99
00310744	**Love Songs**	$12.99
00233740	**The Most Beautiful Songs for Easy Classical Piano**	$12.99
00220036	**Pop Ballads**	$14.99
00311406	**Pop Gems of the 1950s**	$12.95
00311407	**Pop Gems of the 1960s**	$12.95
00233739	**Pop Standards for Easy Classical Piano**	$12.99
00102887	**A Ragtime Christmas**	$12.99
00311293	**Ragtime Classics**	$10.95
00312028	**Santa Swings**	$12.99
00233688	**Songs from Childhood for Easy Classical Piano**	$12.99
00103258	**Songs of Inspiration**	$12.99
00310840	**Sweet Land of Liberty**	$12.99
00126450	**10,000 Reasons**	$14.99
00310712	**Timeless Praise**	$12.95
00311086	**TV Themes**	$12.99
00310717	**21 Great Classics**	$12.99
00160076	**Waltzes & Polkas for Easy Classical Piano**	$12.99
00145342	**Weekly Worship**	$16.99

BIG-NOTE PIANO

00310838	**Children's Favorite Movie Songs**	$12.99
00346000	**Christmas Movie Magic**	$12.99
00277368	**Classical Favorites**	$12.99
00310907	**Contemporary Hits**	$12.99
00277370	**Disney Favorites**	$14.99
00310888	**Joy to the World**	$12.99
00310908	**The Nutcracker**	$12.99
00277371	**Star Wars**	$16.99

BEGINNING PIANO SOLOS

00311202	**Awesome God**	$12.99
00310837	**Christian Children's Favorites**	$12.99
00311117	**Christmas Traditions**	$10.99
00311250	**Easy Hymns**	$12.99
00102710	**Everlasting God**	$10.99
00311403	**Jazzy Tunes**	$10.95
00310822	**Kids' Favorites**	$12.99
00338175	**Silly Songs for Kids**	$9.99

PIANO DUET

00126452	**The Christmas Variations**	$12.99
00311350	**Classical Theme Duets**	$10.99
00295099	**Gospel Duets**	$12.99
00311544	**Hymn Duets**	$14.99
00311203	**Praise & Worship Duets**	$12.99
00294755	**Sacred Christmas Duets**	$12.99
00119405	**Star Wars**	$14.99
00253545	**Worship Songs for Two**	$12.99

CHRISTMAS COLLECTIONS
FROM HAL LEONARD
ALL BOOKS ARRANGED FOR PIANO, VOICE & GUITAR

THE BEST CHRISTMAS SONGS EVER

69 all-time favorites: Auld Lang Syne • Coventry Carol • Frosty the Snow Man • Happy Holiday • It Came Upon the Midnight Clear • O Holy Night • Rudolph the Red-Nosed Reindeer • Silver Bells • What Child Is This? • and many more.
00359130 ....$29.99

THE BIG BOOK OF CHRISTMAS SONGS

Over 120 all-time favorites and hard-to-find classics: As Each Happy Christmas • The Boar's Head Carol • Carol of the Bells • Deck the Halls • The Friendly Beasts • God Rest Ye Merry Gentlemen • Joy to the World • Masters in This Hall • O Holy Night • Story of the Shepherd • and more.
00311520 ....$22.99

CHRISTMAS SONGS – BUDGET BOOKS

100 holiday favorites: All I Want for Christmas Is You • Christmas Time Is Here • Feliz Navidad • Grandma Got Run Over by a Reindeer • I'll Be Home for Christmas • Last Christmas • O Holy Night • Please Come Home for Christmas • Rockin' Around the Christmas Tree • We Need a Little Christmas • What Child Is This? • and more.
00310887 ....$14.99

CHRISTMAS MOVIE SONGS

34 holiday hits from the big screen: All I Want for Christmas Is You • Believe • Christmas Vacation • Do You Want to Build a Snowman? • Frosty the Snow Man • Have Yourself a Merry Little Christmas • It's Beginning to Look like Christmas • Mele Kalikimaka • Rudolph the Red-Nosed Reindeer • Silver Bells • White Christmas • You're a Mean One, Mr. Grinch • and more.
00146961 ....$19.99

CHRISTMAS PIANO SONGS FOR DUMMIES®

56 favorites: Auld Lang Syne • Away in a Manger • Blue Christmas • The Christmas Song • Deck the Hall • I'll Be Home for Christmas • Jingle Bells • Joy to the World • My Favorite Things • Silent Night • more!
00311387 ....$19.95

CHRISTMAS POP STANDARDS

22 contemporary holiday hits, including: All I Want for Christmas Is You • Christmas Time Is Here • Little Saint Nick • Mary, Did You Know? • Merry Christmas, Darling • Santa Baby • Underneath the Tree • Where Are You Christmas? • and more.
00348998 ....$14.99

CHRISTMAS SING-ALONG

40 seasonal favorites: Away in a Manger • Christmas Time Is Here • Feliz Navidad • Happy Holiday • Jingle Bells • Mary, Did You Know? • O Come, All Ye Faithful • Rudolph the Red-Nosed Reindeer • Silent Night • White Christmas • and more. Includes online sing-along backing tracks.
00278176 Book/Online Audio $24.99

CHRISTMAS SONGS FOR KIDS

28 favorite songs of the season, including: Away in a Manger • Do You Want to Build a Snowman? • Here Comes Santa Claus (Right down Santa Claus Lane) • Mele Kalikimaka • Rudolph the Red-Nosed Reindeer • Santa Claus Is Comin' to Town • Silent Night • Somewhere in My Memory • and many more.
00311571 ....$12.99

100 CHRISTMAS CAROLS

Includes: Away in a Manger • Bring a Torch, Jeannette, Isabella • Coventry Carol • Deck the Hall • The First Noel • Go, Tell It on the Mountain • I Heard the Bells on Christmas Day • Joy to the World • O Come, All Ye Faithful (Adeste Fideles) • Silent Night • Sing We Now of Christmas • and more.
00310897 ....$19.99

100 MOST BEAUTIFUL CHRISTMAS SONGS

Includes: Angels We Have Heard on High • Baby, It's Cold Outside • Christmas Time Is Here • Do You Hear What I Hear • Grown-Up Christmas List • Happy Xmas (War Is Over) • I'll Be Home for Christmas • The Little Drummer Boy • Mary, Did You Know? • O Holy Night • White Christmas • Winter Wonderland • and more.
00237285 ....$24.99

POPULAR CHRISTMAS SHEET MUSIC: 1980-2017

40 recent seasonal favorites: All I Want for Christmas Is You • Because It's Christmas (For All the Children) • Breath of Heaven (Mary's Song) • Christmas Lights • The Christmas Shoes • The Gift • Grown-Up Christmas List • Last Christmas • Santa Tell Me • Snowman • Where Are You Christmas? • Wrapped in Red • and more.
00278089 ....$17.99

A SENTIMENTAL CHRISTMAS BOOK

27 beloved Christmas favorites, including: The Christmas Shoes • The Christmas Song (Chestnuts Roasting on an Open Fire) • Christmas Time Is Here • Grown-Up Christmas List • Have Yourself a Merry Little Christmas • I'll Be Home for Christmas • Somewhere in My Memory • Where Are You Christmas? • and more.
00236830 ....$14.99

ULTIMATE CHRISTMAS

100 seasonal favorites: Auld Lang Syne • Bring a Torch, Jeannette, Isabella • Carol of the Bells • The Chipmunk Song • Christmas Time Is Here • The First Noel • Frosty the Snow Man • Gesù Bambino • Happy Holiday • Happy Xmas (War Is Over) • Jingle-Bell Rock • Pretty Paper • Silver Bells • Suzy Snowflake • and more.
00361399 ....$24.99

A VERY MERRY CHRISTMAS

39 familiar favorites: Blue Christmas • Feliz Navidad • Happy Xmas (War Is Over) • I'll Be Home for Christmas • Jingle-Bell Rock • Please Come Home for Christmas • Rockin' Around the Christmas Tree • Santa, Bring My Baby Back (To Me) • Sleigh Ride • White Christmas • and more.
00310536 ....$14.99

Complete contents listings available online at
www.halleonard.com

PRICES, CONTENTS, AND AVAILABILITY SUBJECT TO CHANGE WITHOUT NOTICE.

YOUR FAVORITE MUSIC
ARRANGED FOR PIANO SOLO

    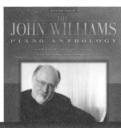 

ARTIST, COMPOSER, TV & MOVIE SONGBOOKS

Adele for Piano Solo
00307585.............................. $17.99

The Beatles Piano Solo
00294023.............................. $17.99

A Charlie Brown Christmas
00313176.............................. $17.99

Paul Cardall – The Hymns Collection
00295925.............................. $24.99

Coldplay for Piano Solo
00307637.............................. $17.99

Selections from Final Fantasy
00148699.............................. $19.99

Alexis Ffrench – The Sheet Music Collection
00345258.............................. $19.99

Game of Thrones
00199166.............................. $17.99

Hamilton
00345612.............................. $19.99

Hillsong Worship Favorites
00303164.............................. $12.99

How to Train Your Dragon
00138210.............................. $19.99

Elton John Collection
00306040.............................. $22.99

La La Land
00283691.............................. $14.99

John Legend Collection
00233195.............................. $17.99

Les Misérables
00290271.............................. $19.99

Little Women
00338470.............................. $19.99

Outlander: The Series
00254460.............................. $19.99

The Peanuts® Illustrated Songbook
00313178.............................. $24.99

Astor Piazzolla – Piano Collection
00285510.............................. $17.99

Pirates of the Caribbean – Curse of the Black Pearl
00313256.............................. $19.99

Pride & Prejudice
00123854.............................. $17.99

Queen
00289784.............................. $19.99

John Williams Anthology
00194555.............................. $24.99

George Winston Piano Solos
00306822.............................. $22.99

MIXED COLLECTIONS

Beautiful Piano Instrumentals
00149926.............................. $16.99

Best Jazz Piano Solos Ever
00312079.............................. $24.99

Best Piano Solos Ever
00242928.............................. $19.99

Big Book of Classical Music
00310508.............................. $19.99

Big Book of Ragtime Piano
00311749.............................. $22.99

Christmas Medleys
00350572.............................. $16.99

Disney Medleys
00242588.............................. $17.99

Disney Piano Solos
00313128.............................. $17.99

Favorite Pop Piano Solos
00312523.............................. $16.99

Great Piano Solos
00311273.............................. $16.99

The Greatest Video Game Music
00201767.............................. $19.99

Most Relaxing Songs
00233879.............................. $17.99

Movie Themes Budget Book
00289137.............................. $14.99

100 of the Most Beautiful Piano Solos Ever
00102787.............................. $29.99

100 Movie Songs
00102804.............................. $29.99

Peaceful Piano Solos
00286009.............................. $17.99

Piano Solos for All Occasions
00310964.............................. $24.99

River Flows in You & Other Eloquent Songs
00123854.............................. $17.99

Sunday Solos for Piano
00311272.............................. $17.99

Top Hits for Piano Solo
00294635.............................. $14.99

HAL•LEONARD®

View songlists online and order from your favorite music retailer at
halleonard.com

0621
195

Prices, content, and availability subject to change without notice.

Disney characters and artwork TM & © 2021 Disney